SCHIRMER'S LIBRARY
OF MUSICAL CLASSICS

Vol. 2012

ALEXANDER SCRIABIN

Keyboard Essentials
(Original Works)

For Piano

ISBN 978-0-7935-4415-8

G. SCHIRMER, Inc.

DISTRIBUTED BY

HAL•LEONARD®
CORPORATION

7777 W. BLUEMOUND RD. P.O. BOX 13819 MILWAUKEE, WI 53213

CONTENTS

Alexander Scriabin was one of a handful of composers who was able to completely express his style at easier technical levels. Although no Scriabin work is truly for the beginner, the editors have carefully selected works for this volume from among the easiest of Scriabin's short works. They can, therefore, serve as an encyclopedic introduction to the music of Scriabin as well as an all-inclusive preparation for the more difficult short works, and of course, the ten Piano Sonatas.

Within the range of this volume, the selections may be roughly divided into three technical levels:

Easiest	Moderately Challenging	Most Challenging
Impromptu (à la Mazur) Op. 2, No. 3	Mazurka Op. 3, No. 7	Prelude for the Left Hand Op. 9, No. 1
Mazurka Op. 3, No. 2	Prelude Op. 11, No. 2	Prelude Op. 11, No. 3
Mazurka Op. 3, No. 4	Prelude Op. 11, No. 5	Prelude Op. 13, No. 5
Mazurka Op. 3, No. 5	Prelude Op. 11, No. 9	Mazurka Op. 25, No. 6
Prelude Op. 11, No. 4	Prelude Op. 11, No. 13	Prelude Op. 27, No. 2
Prelude Op. 11, No. 15	Prelude Op. 13, No. 1	Prelude Op. 35, No. 3
Prelude Op. 11, No. 17	Prelude Op. 13, No. 3	Etude Op. 42, No. 3
Prelude Op. 11, No. 21	Prelude Op. 16, No. 3	Poeme Op. 44, No. 1
Prelude Op. 11, No. 22	Prelude Op. 16, No. 4	Poème Fantasque Op. 45, No. 2
	Prelude Op. 22, No. 3	Rêverie Op. 49, No. 3
	Mazurka Op. 25, No. 1	Prelude Op. 51, No. 2
	Mazurka Op. 25, No. 3	Poème Ailé Op. 51, No. 3
	Prelude Op. 39, No. 1	Danse Languide Op. 51, No. 4
	Mazurka Op. 40, No. 1	Enigme Op. 52, No. 2
	Mazurka Op. 40, No. 2	Nuances Op. 56, No. 3
	Feuillet D'Album Op. 45, No. 1	Caresse Dansée Op. 57, No. 2
		Etude Op. 65, No. 2
		Prelude Op. 67, No. 1
		Guirlands Op. 73, No. 1
		Prelude Op. 74, No. 2
		Prelude Op. 74, No. 4

ALEXANDER SCRIABIN (1872–1915) received the gold medal in piano from the Moscow Conservatory, where he also studied composition. Like his schoolmate, Sergei Rachmaninov, he embarked on a successful dual career as composer and piano virtuoso. His concert activity took him all over Europe and to the United States. Unlike Rachmaninov, Scriabin had small hands; he could span no more than an octave comfortably.

The music of Chopin exerted the strongest influence on the young Scriabin, which is reflected both in the style of his early piano works and in his choice of titles (preludes, impromptus, mazurkas). Gradually, the harmonic and melodic language of his music evolved in a unique and original direction. Traditional tonality was left behind, replaced by a harmonic logic based predominantly on complex fourth chords and invented scales.

The change in musical style was mirrored by an increasing absorption, after 1903, with mystical philosophies and with Scriabin's attempt to embody them in his music. The introduction of the interplay of colored lights in the score of the orchestral "Prometheus, The Poem of Fire" (1911) represented only a preliminary step towards his vision of the cosmic fusion of all the forces of art and nature. The ultimate realization of this cataclysmic synthesis, the "Mysterium," was left incomplete at Scriabin's untimely death.

—LAUREL E. FAY

IMPROMPTU
(à la Mazur)
Op. 2, No. 3

Alexander Scriabin

MAZURKA
Op. 3, No. 2

Allegretto non tanto

rit.　　　　a tempo

MAZURKA
Op. 3, No. 4

Moderato

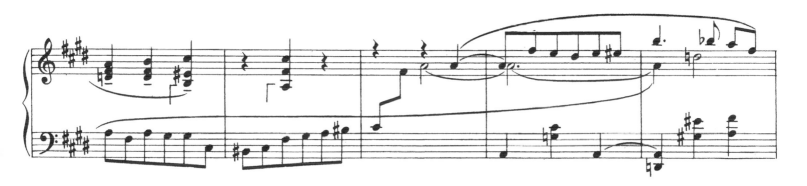

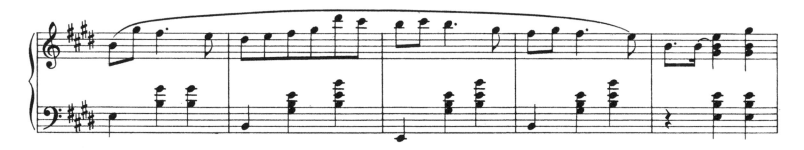

7

Grazioso *rubato*

p   *espr.*

f

MAZURKA
Op. 3, No. 5

Doloroso *poco rubato*

1) *con sordino*

1) i.e., una corda

12

MAZURKA
Op. 3, No. 7

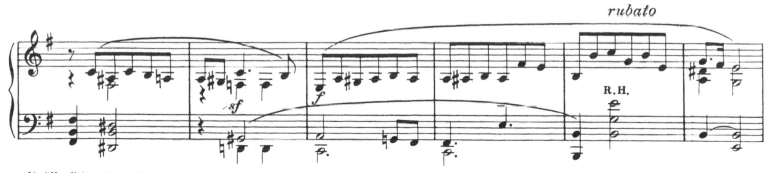

1) All editions have E—B—E in the left hand, but compare with measure 10.

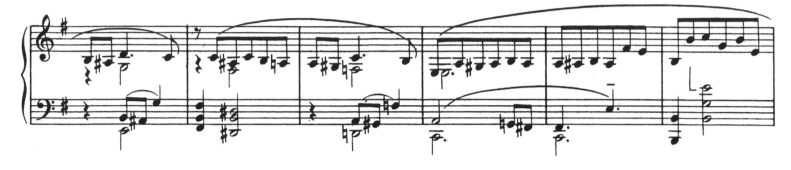

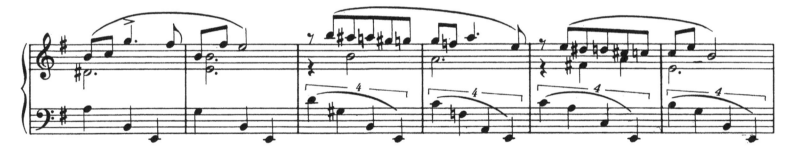

PRELUDE
for the Left Hand
Op. 9, No. 1

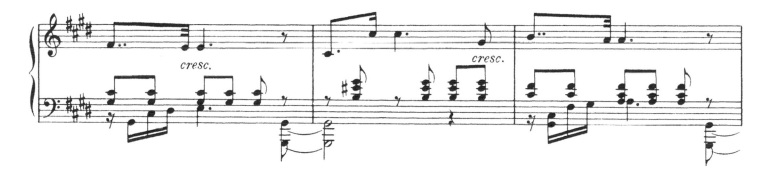

PRELUDE
Op. 11, No. 2

accel. rit.

rit.

PRELUDE
Op. 11, No. 3

Vivo ♩ = 184 - 192 - 200

PRELUDE
Op. 11, No. 4

PRELUDE
Op. 11, No. 5

PRELUDE
Op. 11, No. 9

Andantino ♩ = 66

PRELUDE
Op. 11, No. 13

PRELUDE
Op. 11, No. 15

PRELUDE
Op. 11, No. 17

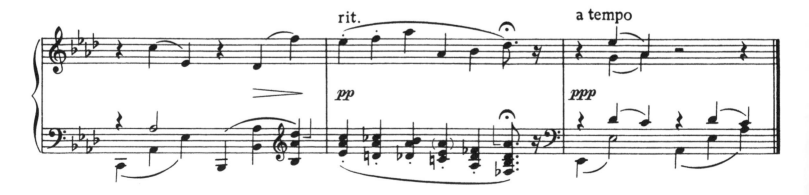

PRELUDE
Op. 11, No. 21

1) Scriabin himself began the *pp* on the third quarter note.

PRELUDE
Op. 11, No. 22

Lento ♩ = 76
rubato

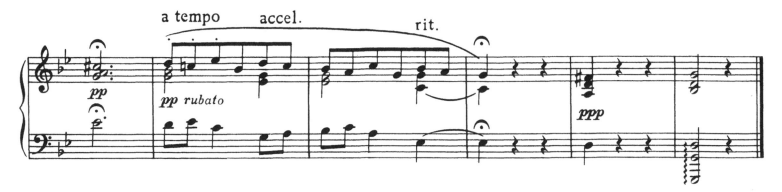

1) Scriabin often played the last chord in this measure *f*, followed by an immediate *pp* in the following bar, yielding an echo effect.

PRELUDE
Op. 13, No. 1

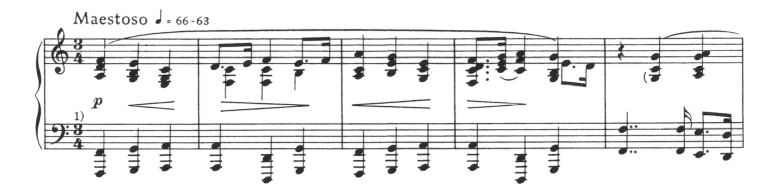

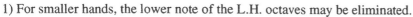

1) For smaller hands, the lower note of the L.H. octaves may be eliminated.

1) Easier: these L.H. chords may be omitted in the next four bars.

PRELUDE
Op. 13, No. 3

PRELUDE
Op. 13, No. 5

Allegro ♩. = 116-120

PRELUDE
Op. 16, No. 3

Andante cantabile ♩= 63

PRELUDE
Op. 16, No. 4

PRELUDE
Op. 22, No. 3

Allegretto M.M. ♩ = 152

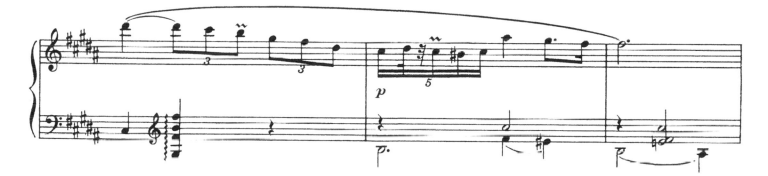

MAZURKA
Op. 25, No. 1

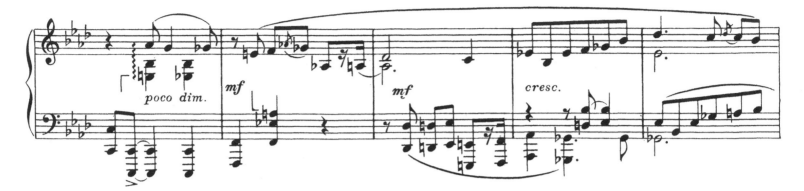

Vivace scherzando

poco rit.

a tempo

poco rit.

Tempo I

L.H.(over)

MAZURKA
Op. 25, No. 3

poco rit.

1) The arpeggio should be played rather slowly.

MAZURKA
Op. 25, No. 6

Più vivo ♩ = 144

52

1) For smaller hands, the lower octave (between the brackets) may be omitted.

PRELUDE
Op. 27, No. 2

PRELUDE
Op. 35, No. 3

Scherzoso ♩.=126

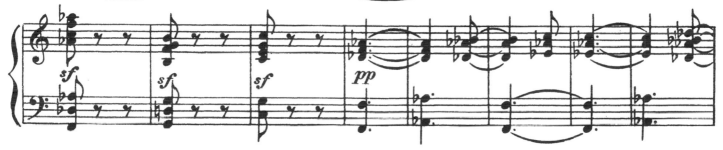

PRELUDE
Op. 39, No. 1

MAZURKA
Op. 40, No. 1

59

1) Those with smaller hands may have to eliminate the middle C altogether.

MAZURKA
Op. 40, No. 2

ETUDE
Op. 42, No. 3

Prestissimo ♩.= 76

POEME
Op. 44, No. 1

FEUILLET D'ALBUM
Op. 45, No. 1

Andante piacevole ♩ = 108

POÈME FANTASQUE
Op. 45, No. 2

RÊVERIE
Op. 49, No. 3

PRELUDE
Op. 51, No. 2

Lugubre

POÈME AILÉ
Op. 51, No. 3

DANSE LANGUIDE
Op. 51, No. 4

ENIGME
Op. 52, No. 2

Etrange, capricieusement

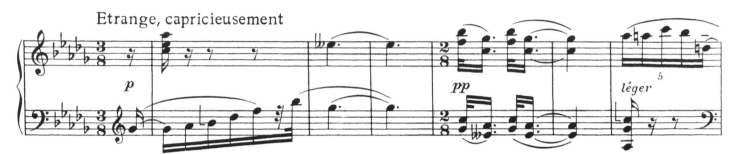

Voluptueux, charmé

NUANCES
Op. 56, No. 3

Blurred, velvety

CARESSE DANSÉE
Op. 57, No. 2

ETUDE
Op. 65, No. 2

Tempo I

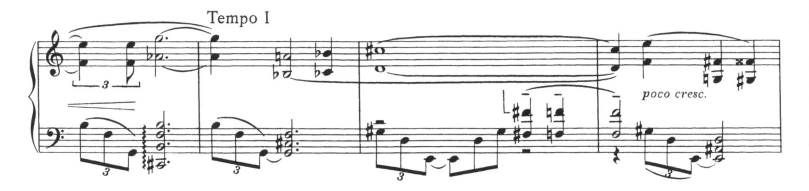

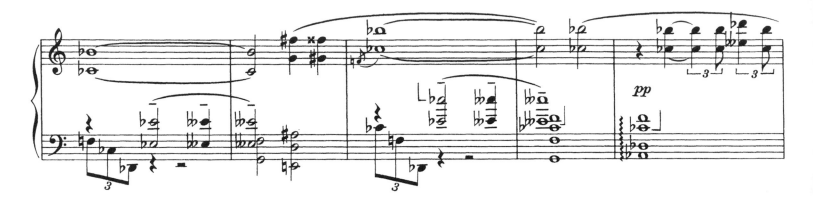

molto accel.

presto volando

PRELUDE
Op. 67, No. 1

Andante

pp vague, mystérieux

déchirant

molto accel.   molto ritard.

GUIRLANDS
Op. 73, No. 1

With a langorous grace

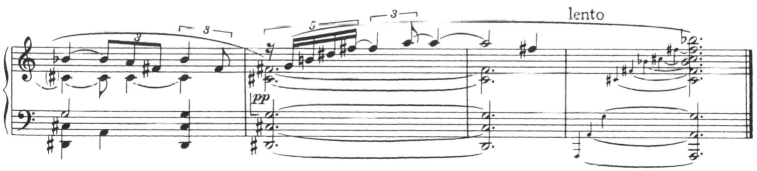

PRELUDE
Op. 74, No. 2

Très lent, contemplatif

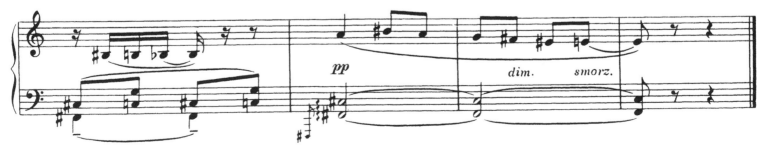

PRELUDE
Op. 74, No. 4

Lent, vague, indécis